MAYER SMITH

Lovers Between the Stars

First edition

This book was professionally typeset on Reedsy.
Find out more at reedsy.com

Contents

One

A Love Written in the Stars

The silence of space was absolute, a vast and endless void that stretched beyond the limits of imagination. It was both haunting and beautiful, an unspoken promise of discovery and destruction. Celeste Arden had spent years preparing for this mission, but nothing could prepare her for the weightless solitude that came with floating among the stars.

She drifted through the dimly lit corridors of the Stellar Dawn, her fingers brushing against the cold metal walls for balance. Outside the viewing panels, the exoplanet V-616C loomed in the distance, its surface an expanse of swirling indigo storms and obsidian ridges. A planet untouched, unexplored—a place that could redefine humanity's understanding of the universe.

If they made it back.

Celeste exhaled slowly, steadying her breath as she approached the research bay. The ship's artificial intelligence, V.E.G.A, hummed faintly through the speakers embedded in the walls. "Dr. Arden," the voice was smooth, almost too human. "You are awake earlier than your scheduled cycle. Do you require assistance?"

"No, I just—" she hesitated, glancing toward the security monitor. "I thought I heard something."

"A distortion in the communications frequency was detected an hour ago," V.E.G.A replied. "No anomalies have been found aboard."

Celeste frowned. It wasn't like her to be paranoid, but something felt off. A prickling at the back of her neck, a sensation like being watched even though the crew was small, and the station was sealed tight. She pushed the thought aside and entered the research bay.

The soft glow of holographic screens flickered to life as she approached her workstation. Data from the planet's atmosphere streamed across the interface—high methane levels, erratic pressure shifts, and signs of subterranean heat pockets that hinted at volcanic activity beneath the surface.

It was everything she had dreamed of studying. And yet, for the first time in her life, the unknown did not excite her. It unsettled her.

A shadow moved behind her.

She turned sharply, heart hammering.

"Relax, Doc," a deep voice drawled. "Didn't mean to startle you."

Orion Vale stood a few feet away, his tall frame silhouetted against the ambient glow of the screens. His dark flight suit clung to his athletic build, the standard issue uniform somehow looking more natural on him than anyone else aboard. A few strands of his raven-black hair had fallen over his forehead, and his piercing green eyes locked onto hers with an intensity that made her stomach tighten.

"How do you always move so quietly?" she asked, forcing her voice to steady.

Orion smirked, leaning against the edge of a nearby console. "Pilots learn to be light on their feet. Comes with the job."

Celeste exhaled, shaking her head. "You could give a person a heart attack."

He lifted an eyebrow. "Didn't take you for the nervous type."

"I'm not," she said too quickly.

"Then what's got you on edge?"

Celeste hesitated. He would think she was being ridiculous. She barely understood it herself—this strange sense of something lurking just beneath the surface of reality, like a signal too faint to hear but present nonetheless.

Instead of answering, she turned back to her research, scrolling through the planetary data. "Couldn't sleep."

Orion didn't respond immediately, but she could feel his gaze lingering on her. He always watched her like that—not with judgment, but with the quiet curiosity of a man who had seen too much yet still wanted to understand the world around him.

Or understand her.

"Long night for a scientist," he mused.

She gave him a sideways glance. "Says the pilot wandering the halls instead of resting before tomorrow's planetary descent."

He let out a soft chuckle, but it didn't reach his eyes. "Didn't feel like sleeping."

Celeste knew better than to pry. Orion was not the kind of man who let his guard down easily. He carried secrets the way others carried scars, visible only in the way his jaw tightened when certain topics arose or in the fleeting shadows that passed across his face when he thought no one was looking.

Instead, she changed the subject. "I found something unusual in the ship's system logs earlier."

Orion straightened slightly. "What kind of unusual?"

Celeste tapped a few keys, pulling up the encrypted file she had stumbled upon hours ago. It wasn't part of the standard reports or mission records. The metadata suggested it had been accessed recently—too recently for comfort.

"Someone's been modifying logs in the mainframe," she said. "I don't know who, but this file—" She gestured toward the fragmented data. "It's encoded with an old encryption model. Almost like someone didn't want it to be noticed."

Orion's expression darkened as he leaned closer. "Did you open it?"

"I tried, but it's locked behind layers of security. I don't have the clearance to override it."

"Let me see." Orion's fingers moved across the console with practiced ease. His time as a pilot meant he had access to more ship systems than she did, and as she watched him navigate the encryption, she realized just how adept he was at maneuvering through classified data.

Minutes passed in silence, the only sound the quiet hum of the ship around them. Then, Orion muttered a curse under his breath.

"What?" Celeste asked.

He leaned back, tension tightening his features. "It's not just modified logs. These are redacted mission reports."

Her pulse quickened. "From our mission?"

"No." His voice was grim. "From past missions. Ones that never returned."

A cold wave of dread washed over her.

Celeste had read about failed expeditions, but official records claimed they were lost to mechanical failures, unexpected planetary conditions—explainable accidents. But this… this was something else.

"Why would they hide this?" she whispered.

Orion's gaze met hers, and for the first time since she had met him, she saw something almost like fear in his eyes.

"Because," he murmured, "someone doesn't want us to know what really happened."

A faint shudder ran through the ship, subtle but noticeable. The lights flickered, and in the brief moment of darkness, a static-laced voice crackled through the comm system.

Celeste's breath hitched.

Orion tensed.

Then, the message played.

"Some truths are meant to be lost in the stars."

The voice cut out. The lights stabilized. The ship returned to its usual hum, as if nothing had happened.

But Celeste knew, in that moment, that everything had changed.

She and Orion were not alone in their search for answers.

And whatever was out there—whatever was watching them—wanted them to stop.

Two

Whispers in the Void

The rhythmic pulse of the Stellar Dawn was like the heartbeat of a living entity, steady and unyielding as it drifted through the cold void of space. But to Celeste Arden, it felt more like a trap. The hum of the engines reverberated through the steel walls, the low vibration a constant reminder that she was far from the world she knew, locked in an endless expanse of stars, surrounded by the unknown.

She stood in front of the observation deck, her palms pressed against the glass as she watched the swirling atmosphere of V-616C. The planet was a study in contradictions: violent storms tearing across its surface while hidden beneath, an eerie stillness beckoned. It was as if the planet were alive, breathing—waiting for something. But Celeste could not escape the gnawing feeling that it was not the planet that unsettled her. It was something aboard the ship.

Or, more precisely, someone.

Orion Vale had been absent from the research bay for the past few hours, and for the first time, she found herself missing his presence. It was odd, she thought, to feel that way about a man she hardly knew. He wasn't the type to wear his emotions on his sleeve, yet there was something about him that drew her in. Something dangerous, yet magnetic. He had a way of watching her, his gaze intense and unwavering, as though searching for a secret she hadn't told him, but was certain he already knew.

She exhaled sharply, brushing her hair from her face. Her thoughts were starting to spiral again. She needed clarity—something solid to hold onto.

"Dr. Arden." The soft voice of V.E.G.A echoed through the room, smooth and emotionless.

Celeste didn't turn. "Yes, V.E.G.A?"

"The encrypted file you requested is still under review. No unauthorized access has been detected."

"I didn't ask for a status update."

"Your request is noted."

"Stop reading my mind." Celeste muttered, half-smiling despite herself.

It was an idle joke, but the AI's persistent monitoring made it feel more like an invasion. It had a way of inserting itself into her thoughts when she least expected it.

There was a soft swish of movement behind her, a fleeting sound that tugged at her attention. She spun around, heart hammering in her chest, her pulse quickening at the sudden presence.

Orion stood there, leaning against the doorframe, arms crossed over his chest. He had a habit of slipping in and out of spaces without a sound, and it was something that both irritated and intrigued her. His expression was unreadable, as always, but there was a tension in his jaw, a tautness in his posture.

"Didn't mean to startle you," he said, his voice low, almost too soft for the space.

Celeste's breath caught in her throat. "I thought you were…"

"Gone?" He gave a small, almost imperceptible smile. "I don't sleep much."

"Right." She turned back to the window, the need for distance in her voice betraying her growing unease. "What brings you here?"

Orion stepped closer, the shift in the air around him almost tangible. She could smell the faint hint of coffee and engine grease on his clothes, a strange juxtaposition to the sterile, antiseptic scent of the station.

"I came to check on you," he said, his voice edged with an unfamiliar seriousness. "You've been off ever since we found that file."

Celeste's shoulders stiffened, but she refused to look at him. "I'm fine." The words were clipped, but she didn't trust them.

He didn't respond immediately, but she could feel his presence behind her, unwavering and intense. "You're not." His voice was softer now, almost as if he were speaking to himself. "You've been digging into things you shouldn't."

The statement hung between them like a charged particle, just waiting to explode. She could feel the weight of his words pressing down on her, but she refused to give in to the tension. She wasn't the kind of woman to be easily intimidated.

"You're one to talk," she finally said, her voice barely above a whisper. "You've been hiding your own secrets from the moment I met you."

Orion's breath caught, but he didn't step back. His presence seemed to grow even more overwhelming as he closed the distance between them.

"I didn't come here to talk about me."

"No, you never do." Celeste's words were sharp, but she felt a flutter of unease in her chest. Was she trying to push him away, or was she trying to prove to herself that she could remain unaffected by him? It was hard to tell anymore.

Orion stood behind her, his breath warm against her neck. She felt the warmth of his body, his proximity almost too intimate, yet she didn't want to pull away. There was something magnetic about him, something that called to her despite the warning bells ringing in her mind.

Her pulse quickened as he reached out, fingers brushing her shoulder. The touch was light, almost accidental, but it felt like a spark had ignited between them, a connection that defied logic. She should have stepped back, should have pulled away from the intensity of his gaze, but she couldn't.

"I don't know what you're looking for, Celeste," Orion murmured, his voice softer now, as though speaking to her alone in the vastness of space. "But sometimes, you need to stop looking and start listening."

The words hit her like a physical blow, and for a moment, the weight of his presence was too much to bear. She turned to face him, her breath catching in her throat. His eyes, that piercing shade of green, were locked on hers, filled with a quiet understanding. It was as if he could see straight through her, peeling back layers she wasn't ready to expose.

"What do you mean?" she whispered.

He didn't answer immediately. Instead, he reached up, brushing a loose strand of hair from her face with the gentleness of someone who understood the fragility of the moment.

"I mean," he said, his voice barely a whisper now, "sometimes the answers are right in front of you."

Her heart skipped a beat as his fingers lingered at her cheek, his touch sending a jolt of warmth through her skin. She should have pulled away—she knew she should—but something about him held her in place.

There was a moment of silence, pregnant with unspoken words. A tension, thick and charged, hung between them. Then, just as quickly as the moment had come, it was gone.

Orion stepped back, his hands slipping into the pockets of his flight suit. "I'll let you get back to your research."

Celeste stood frozen, her mind racing as he turned and walked toward the door. Her heart was still pounding in her chest, the echo of his touch still lingering on her skin. She hadn't expected him to leave—she didn't want him to leave.

But Orion was already gone.

The door hissed shut behind him, and Celeste was left standing in the quiet of the observation room, her thoughts swirling like the storm on the distant planet. She didn't know what was happening between them, but she could feel it—a shift in the air, an undeniable pull.

And yet, deep down, she knew this wasn't just about them.

There was something much larger at play here. Something that reached beyond their fragile connection.

The encrypted file. The mysterious disappearances. The warning that echoed through her mind, louder than ever: Some truths are meant to be lost in the stars.

14

Three

The Missing Navigator

The morning cycle aboard the Stellar Dawn was marked by the artificial glow of the overhead lights, flickering to simulate the slow rise of a distant sun. The station's automated systems hummed in a rhythmic pattern, a sound so constant that it had become part of the crew's subconscious. But today, something was different. Today, the usual order of things felt… disrupted.

Celeste Arden sensed it the moment she stepped out of her quarters. It was the silence—an eerie, unnatural stillness that pressed against her skin like an invisible weight. Normally, the corridors would echo with the sound of crew members exchanging reports, boots clanking against the reinforced floors, the occasional laugh or groan of exhaustion. But now, the hallways were empty.

She glanced up at the security panel embedded in the wall. The system logs showed no irregularities, but she knew better than to trust appearances. Something had shifted in the night cycle— something she couldn't quite put her finger on.

Her unease only deepened as she reached the mess hall. Orion was already there, standing near the entrance, his stance rigid, his expression unreadable. He hadn't touched the food on the tray in front of him. Instead, he was focused on Captain Elias Shaw, who stood near the center of the room, his arms crossed tightly over his chest. The captain's face was hard, his sharp features set in a grim scowl.

Celeste barely had time to process the tension in the air before she noticed that one of the crew was missing.

Rhys Calloway, the navigator.

She scanned the room, searching for the tall, lanky man who was usually the first to start the day's work. But his seat was empty, his usual sarcastic quips absent. She turned back to Orion, who met her gaze with a slight shake of his head.

Something was wrong.

"Alright," Captain Shaw's voice cut through the silence. "Someone tell me why Calloway missed the morning check-in."

A murmur passed between the remaining crew members. Dr. Elara Voss, the ship's medical officer, shifted uncomfortably in her seat, her blue eyes flickering with hesitation. "I went by his quarters," she said finally. "There was no answer."

"Did you override the door?" Shaw asked, his tone sharper than usual.

Elara nodded. "Yes. He wasn't there."

The words settled over the room like a suffocating fog.

Celeste felt her stomach tighten. A missing crew member wasn't just an inconvenience—it was an anomaly. On a ship like this, where every movement was logged, where every door required access codes, people didn't just disappear.

Unless someone wanted them to.

Shaw turned to V.E.G.A., his voice cutting through the silence. "Pull Calloway's logs. Last known location."

The AI responded immediately, its voice smooth and unbothered by the rising tension. "Lieutenant Calloway's last recorded entry was at 22:43 hours in the navigation bay. No further movements detected."

"That's not possible," Celeste blurted out before she could stop herself.

Shaw's sharp gaze snapped toward her. "Explain."

Celeste swallowed. "There are cameras everywhere. Sensors. If he left the navigation bay, there should be a record of it. If he didn't leave…" She hesitated, the implications too disturbing to voice.

Orion finished for her. "Then he vanished inside the ship."

A chilling silence followed.

Celeste's pulse thrummed in her ears. Orion's words weren't just speculation. He was saying exactly what she had been thinking since the moment she walked into the room. Someone had erased Rhys Calloway.

"V.E.G.A.," Shaw said again, his voice controlled but laced with tension. "Replay the navigation bay footage from last night."

A small holographic projection flickered to life in the center of the mess hall. The grainy feed showed Rhys at his station, his fingers gliding over the console. He looked tired, but there was nothing out of the ordinary. For several minutes, he worked in silence, checking flight trajectories, adjusting star maps.

Then, without warning, the screen glitched.

The image distorted, breaking into fractured pixels. A burst of white noise hissed through the speakers, and when the feed stabilized a second later—Rhys was gone.

Celeste's breath hitched.

One moment, he had been there. The next, the chair sat empty, the console lights flickering as if nothing had happened.

"That's not a camera malfunction," Orion said quietly.

Celeste agreed. If it had been a simple glitch, the footage would have resumed where it left off. But the logs acted as though Rhys had never existed at all.

Shaw's jaw clenched. "Could someone have tampered with the feed?"

Orion crossed his arms. "It's possible. But if they did, they'd have to override the system at the highest level."

"All access requests are logged," V.E.G.A. added. "No unauthorized activity has been detected."

Celeste's stomach churned. "That's not right. Someone had to do this. People don't just… disappear."

Elara spoke up, her voice barely above a whisper. "Maybe he left the ship."

Orion turned to her, his expression unreadable. "How? The airlock logs are clean. No departures. No suits missing."

A cold realization settled over the room.

Rhys Calloway had not left the ship.

He had been erased from it.

Shaw's gaze swept over the gathered crew. He was a man of

logic, a captain who believed in control, in systems, in order. But even he couldn't ignore what had just unfolded before them.

"Until we find out what happened," he said slowly, "no one goes anywhere alone. Understood?"

Nods of agreement passed around the room, though the fear in everyone's eyes was unmistakable.

Celeste felt the weight of Orion's stare and turned to meet his gaze. His eyes were dark, filled with something unreadable. This wasn't an accident, and they both knew it.

Orion leaned in slightly, his voice barely above a whisper. "This is just the beginning."

A shiver ran down Celeste's spine.

For the first time since stepping onto the Stellar Dawn, she felt something she had never expected to feel among the stars.

Fear.

Four

Zero Gravity

The search for Rhys Calloway turned up nothing.

The crew had scoured every inch of the Stellar Dawn, their voices crackling through the comms as they combed through corridors, airlocks, supply compartments—anywhere a man could reasonably (or unreasonably) be. And yet, there was no sign of him. No personal effects left in his quarters, no fingerprints where they should have been. As if he had never existed at all.

Celeste Arden couldn't shake the feeling that something was watching them. A pressure in the air, an electric pulse beneath her skin that kept her on edge. Every breath felt heavier, every shadow stretched just a little too long.

She floated weightlessly in the central maintenance shaft,

tethered by only a thin safety harness as she examined the station's power grid. The flickering lights in the navigation bay had suggested an anomaly in the system, and if there was any chance that Rhys's disappearance was connected, she needed to know.

The soft hum of the station surrounded her, punctuated by the rhythmic beeping of her diagnostic scanner. Celeste's gloved fingers brushed against the cold metal panels as she navigated the intricate circuits, her mind racing.

"V.E.G.A.," she said, her voice steady but clipped. "Run a secondary diagnostic on all system logs for the last twenty-four hours. Look for anything that was deleted or altered."

A beat of silence. Then, the AI responded.

"There are no missing logs, Dr. Arden. The records are intact."

Celeste's stomach tightened. "That's impossible. There has to be something—"

A loud snap echoed through the shaft, and suddenly, Celeste's world lurched.

The safety harness detached from the wall.

She barely had time to react before she was weightless, floating helplessly in the tight, metallic tunnel. Her hands scrambled for something—anything—to grab onto, but there was nothing but open space.

Her heartbeat pounded in her ears.

"V.E.G.A!" she gasped. "Emergency tether—"

The comms crackled. Static.

Then, another voice. His voice.

"Hold on!"

A hand shot out from the maintenance hatch above her, fingers closing around her wrist in a firm grip. The momentum of the sudden grasp sent them both spinning in the confined space, the force of it sending Celeste colliding into the solid warmth of Orion Vale's chest.

For a moment, everything stopped.

They floated together in the narrow corridor, suspended in the weightlessness of space, their bodies tangled as they adjusted to the sudden stillness.

Celeste's breath came out ragged, her fingers still wrapped around Orion's arm as she fought the dizzying sensation of nearly being lost in the void. His grip on her waist was strong, anchoring her.

She was close enough to see the flecks of gold in his green eyes, the way his dark lashes framed them. Close enough to feel the slight hitch in his breath.

"You okay?" His voice was low, barely more than a whisper.

Celeste swallowed hard. "You—" She exhaled, trying to slow her racing heart. "You caught me."

Orion gave her a small, knowing smirk. "You sound surprised."

"I—" Her thoughts were scrambled, jumbled by the adrenaline still surging through her veins. "The safety tether detached."

"I know," he murmured. "That wasn't an accident."

Her pulse spiked. "What do you mean?"

Orion didn't answer immediately. Instead, he reached out with his free hand and grabbed a stabilizing rail, pulling them both toward the nearest hatch. The motion brought them even closer, their bodies brushing against each other in the slow, fluid movements dictated by zero gravity.

Celeste's mind screamed at her to focus on the implications of his words—that someone had deliberately compromised her safety. But at that moment, all she could focus on was the way Orion was looking at her. The way his fingers lingered against her waist just a fraction of a second longer than necessary.

She felt her breath catch, the unspoken weight of something between them stretching thin, fragile.

"You saved me," she said softly.

Orion exhaled sharply, his grip on her waist tightening just slightly. "I wasn't about to let you drift into the maintenance grid." His voice was quiet, but there was an edge to it. Something deeper.

Something that sent a different kind of shiver down her spine.

Celeste knew she should move, should put space between them, should say something logical—but she couldn't. Not when his eyes were locked on hers like that, studying her as if he were trying to memorize every detail.

The moment stretched impossibly long. The artificial glow of the maintenance lights flickered around them, casting soft shadows across his face.

Then, without thinking, without meaning to, she leaned in.

Orion's breath hitched, and for a split second, Celeste saw hesitation flicker across his features. A battle.

But he didn't move away.

He closed the distance.

Their lips met in the weightlessness of the corridor, the kiss slow and uncertain at first, as if both were testing the limits of the moment. But then, something shifted.

The tension that had been building between them for days ignited, and the kiss deepened. Celeste felt Orion's hand slide from her waist to the small of her back, pulling her closer, eliminating the space between them entirely.

It was nothing like she had expected.

It was intense, charged, like a supernova waiting to explode.

Celeste's fingers found their way to the back of his neck, her heart hammering against her ribcage as she let herself get lost in the sensation of it—the warmth of his lips, the quiet hunger beneath the surface.

Then—

The lights flickered violently.

A cold voice crackled through the comms, shattering the fragile moment.

"Dr. Arden. Orion Vale. You are not alone."

A chill ran down Celeste's spine.

Orion pulled back, his expression instantly sharp, his hand instinctively moving toward the knife strapped to his belt.

Celeste barely had time to process what had just happened before the corridor plunged into darkness.

Then—an unnatural click.

A sound that did not belong in the sterile silence of space.

Something was inside the station with them.

Celeste's breath came fast, her mind shifting from the lingering heat of the kiss to raw survival instinct. Orion's hand found hers in the darkness, his grip tight.

"Move," he whispered.

And together, they pushed off from the maintenance shaft, the warmth of their stolen moment already fading into the cold reality of what awaited them next.

Five

Ghosts in the System

Darkness swallowed the corridor.

Celeste Arden's breath came in rapid bursts, her fingers still wrapped around Orion Vale's as they floated weightlessly in the sudden abyss. The emergency lights hadn't kicked in. The hum of the Stellar Dawn, always steady, always there, had faltered into an unnatural silence.

Something wasn't just wrong. Something was watching them.

Orion's grip on her tightened, his breath warm and controlled beside her. "Stay close," he whispered, his voice barely more than a vibration in the space between them.

Celeste swallowed hard, forcing herself to focus on the present rather than the lingering sensation of his lips against hers. Their kiss had barely registered before the cold voice on the comms sent ice through her veins.

"You are not alone."

The words still echoed in her mind, taunting her, a whisper in the void.

"V.E.G.A.," she tried, her voice steadier than she felt. "Activate emergency lighting. Respond."

Silence.

The AI wasn't answering.

Orion shifted beside her, bracing against the corridor wall as he pulled a small tactical flashlight from his belt. The narrow beam cut through the darkness, illuminating the stark metallic walls, the tangle of wires snaking along the floor panels, the floating dust particles disturbed by their movements.

Celeste reached for the nearest handrail, steadying herself in the absence of gravity. She had spent years in space, but this—this silence, this stillness—felt alien. Wrong.

"Who do you think that was?" she whispered, though she wasn't sure she wanted the answer.

Orion's jaw tightened. "Not V.E.G.A."

A chill slithered down her spine. "That shouldn't be possible."

Orion didn't reply immediately. Instead, he aimed the flashlight at the maintenance panel beside them. The station's system core access was housed just beyond this point. If there were ghosts in the system, that was where they would be hiding.

"Give me a second," he muttered, reaching for the emergency override.

Celeste stayed close, her gaze darting down the length of the corridor. The absence of sound was suffocating, as if the ship itself was holding its breath.

Then, a sudden thud reverberated from down the hall.

Celeste inhaled sharply, her body going rigid. Orion's flashlight snapped toward the source of the sound.

The maintenance bay.

A faint tapping followed. Slow. Deliberate.

Celeste's pulse hammered against her ribs. It was too precise to be a malfunction. Too controlled to be an accident.

Something was here.

Orion's free hand brushed against her waist, steadying her as they pushed off toward the hatch leading to the maintenance bay. Celeste focused on the faint warmth of his touch, grounding herself in something real. Something human.

The door controls were dead. No power.

Orion didn't hesitate—he reached for his knife, using its edge to pry open the manual release. A hiss of depressurization filled the air as the hatch unlocked, the metal sliding apart.

The beam of his flashlight swept across the darkened bay.

And then Celeste saw it.

Her breath caught.

The words.

Scrawled across the far wall in deep, jagged letters.

"HE NEVER LEFT."

Her stomach lurched.

The writing was uneven, as if scrawled in a rush, in desperation. The strokes were erratic, hurried. And the ink—

No. Not ink.

Blood.

The metallic scent was faint, but unmistakable. The dark smears floated in the weightlessness, tiny droplets suspended in the air, illuminated by Orion's flashlight.

A sickening realization set in.

Rhys Calloway had never left the ship.

"Orion," Celeste whispered, her voice barely audible.

"I see it." His voice was grim, controlled, but she could feel the tension in his grip, the barely restrained fight-or-flight response.

Celeste forced herself to move forward, drifting toward the console near the writing. The terminal flickered—barely powered, its energy fluctuating like a dying heartbeat.

She pressed a few keys. The screen responded sluggishly.

Then, a single message appeared.

FILE RESTRICTED. OVERRIDE REQUIRED.

Another line of text followed, the cursor blinking, as if someone was typing it in real-time.

"SHE CAN'T HELP YOU, ORION."

Celeste's breath hitched.

She whipped around, eyes wide. "What the hell is this?"

Orion was already moving. He grabbed her wrist, yanking her away from the console. "We need to go. Now."

"Who's doing this?" she demanded, but her voice shook. The answer was worse than she wanted to believe.

Someone was inside the system. Someone knew them.

The lights flickered violently, bathing the maintenance bay in bursts of red warning strobes. The comms crackled again, static hissing in her ears.

Then—

A voice. Distorted. Familiar.

"Help me."

Celeste's heart stopped.

It was Rhys Calloway.

Orion's jaw clenched. "That's not him."

Celeste turned back to the terminal, her fingers moving fast, overriding security walls, bypassing the restricted access. The system fought her, resisting her commands, but she was fast.

Finally, the locked file opened.

A garbled video feed appeared on-screen. Static-heavy, distorted. But then—

A figure.

A man floating in the airlock chamber.

Rhys.

But his eyes were open. Wide. Unblinking.

His body was suspended, weightless, his face frozen in an expression of sheer terror.

Then, as if responding to their presence, his head twitched.

A fraction of an inch. A movement that should not have been possible.

Celeste's stomach twisted into knots.

"He's dead," Orion murmured. "That—thing—is not Rhys."

The video feed cut out.

Then, the comms crackled again.

"You should have left it alone."

The emergency lights snapped off.

The ship plunged into darkness.

And in the silence that followed, Celeste heard something.

A breath.

Not hers.

Not Orion's.

Something else.

Something that shouldn't be there.

Something waiting.

Orion's voice was sharp, urgent. "Celeste—"

Before she could react, the airlock doors slammed shut, sealing them inside the maintenance bay.

Then, the whispers began.

Six

The Betrayal Within

The whispers slithered through the darkness.

Celeste Arden could feel them against her skin, crawling over her like unseen hands, pressing into the hollow spaces of her mind. The maintenance bay had become a tomb, the air thick with something unnatural, something unseen. She pressed her back against the cold metal wall, her breath shallow, her pulse hammering against her ribs.

Beside her, Orion Vale's breathing was steady but tense. He was still gripping her wrist, his warmth a stark contrast to the icy terror curling through her veins. His flashlight beam cut through the suffocating dark, but the shadows seemed to move just outside its reach, coiling at the edges like something alive.

Then, the whispering stopped.

Complete silence.

A presence lingered in the air, an oppressive weight pressing down on them, listening. Waiting.

Then—

A metallic scrape echoed from the other side of the maintenance bay.

Celeste stiffened. Orion pulled her closer, his grip firm but careful, his body shifting slightly in front of hers in an instinctive, protective motion.

"Who's there?" Celeste forced the words out, but the ship swallowed them whole.

The only answer was the soft hissing of the life support vents.

Orion reached for his communicator. "V.E.G.A., override security protocols. Open the maintenance bay doors."

Nothing.

The AI was offline.

Orion muttered a curse under his breath. Celeste's mind raced, trying to piece together the impossible. Rhys was dead—she had seen him, suspended in that airlock. But the video feed had moved.

Had he moved?

Or had something else?

A sudden vibration rattled the floor beneath them, so faint it could have been imagined. But Celeste felt it through the soles of her boots, a tremor rippling outward like a breath exhaled from deep within the ship.

Then, from the darkness—

A voice.

"Orion."

Celeste's blood turned to ice.

It was Rhys's voice. But it wasn't coming from the comms. It wasn't mechanical.

It was coming from the room.

Orion's body tensed. The flashlight beam jerked upward, illuminating a dark shape floating just above them—

A body.

Celeste barely had time to register the hollowed-out eyes, the slackened jaw—before the body lurched forward.

Orion shoved her to the side as Rhys Calloway's corpse shot

toward them with unnatural speed. A guttural, wet choking sound escaped from the dead navigator's lips, his limbs moving with a jerky, fractured motion, like a marionette with its strings pulled by an unseen force.

Celeste's scream caught in her throat as she scrambled backward, her hands slipping against the cold metal panels. Orion moved fast—his knife was out in an instant, his reflexes sharp even in zero gravity.

Rhys's corpse lunged.

Orion twisted, catching the body's shoulder and shoving it backward. The impact sent it spinning through the weightless air, its limbs flailing unnaturally.

Then, as suddenly as it had attacked—it stopped.

Suspended in the air, its head tilted at an unnatural angle.

Then, its lips moved.

"You shouldn't be here."

Celeste's breath came fast, her fingers gripping Orion's sleeve, her nails digging into the fabric.

Orion didn't hesitate. He grabbed the emergency panel on the wall and slammed the manual override for the doors. The maintenance bay hatch hissed and groaned as the locks disengaged.

"Move," Orion ordered, his voice sharp, his hand wrapping around Celeste's as he propelled them toward the exit.

The second the doors cracked open, a force pulled them through—

Like an invisible hand shoving them out.

They tumbled into the corridor, the doors slamming shut behind them.

Celeste gasped, clutching Orion's flight suit as the weightless motion slowed. She turned back toward the doors—

Rhys's corpse was still inside. Floating. Motionless.

But his eyes were now locked onto hers.

Then, with a sickening snap—his head twisted backward.

The lights flickered violently, and when the emergency strobes steadied—

He was gone.

Celeste let out a shaking breath, her entire body trembling. "Orion—"

But he wasn't looking at the doors anymore. His eyes were fixed on something further down the hall.

Celeste turned.

And felt her stomach drop.

Captain Shaw and the rest of the crew stood at the end of the corridor, weapons drawn.

The air crackled with tension, the shadows cast by their flashlights making them look like specters in the dim light.

Shaw's voice was cold. "What the hell are you two doing?"

Orion's body was still, unreadable. "Something's in the ship," he said flatly.

Shaw didn't lower his weapon. "Oh, I know. And I want to know why you two seem to be the only ones who keep finding the evidence."

Celeste's heart slammed against her ribs. "You think we—?"

Shaw's jaw clenched. "We have a missing navigator. An altered security feed. And now you two just happen to be locked inside the only bay with a working console?"

Celeste felt a sickening realization snap into place.

The whispers. The corrupted files. The way the system logs had been altered.

Someone had been covering their tracks.

And someone on this crew had the access to do it.

She turned to Orion, her voice barely above a whisper. "This isn't just about Rhys."

Orion nodded, his expression deadly calm. "It's about all of us."

Shaw stepped forward, lowering his weapon slightly but not entirely. "Until we figure out what's going on, you two are confined to quarters."

Celeste opened her mouth to argue, but Orion placed a firm hand on her arm, a silent warning.

Not here. Not now.

Shaw's eyes flicked to Orion. "I know you're hiding something, Vale."

Orion didn't flinch. "And I know you don't trust me. But right now, you have bigger problems than me."

Shaw's jaw tightened. But after a moment, he turned away. "Lock them down," he ordered.

Celeste barely had time to process before two armed crew members stepped forward, ushering them toward the crew quarters.

Orion didn't resist.

Neither did Celeste.

Because for the first time since stepping onto the Stellar Dawn, she wasn't sure who she could trust anymore.

Or if anyone was getting out of this alive.

Seven

Chasing Shadows

The door to Celeste's quarters slammed shut behind her with a finality that sent a shudder down her spine. The mechanical lock engaged with a sharp click, sealing her inside. The small cabin, normally a place of respite, now felt like a cage. The sterile white walls seemed closer, the dim emergency lighting casting long, unsettling shadows.

Orion was locked in the cabin next to hers. They had been separated the moment Shaw's men had marched them down the corridor like criminals.

Celeste's pulse was still hammering in her ears, her breath uneven as she pressed her back against the cold metal of the door. What the hell just happened?

Rhys's corpse had moved.

No—something had moved him.

And now, instead of finding answers, she and Orion were being treated as suspects.

Her hands balled into fists. Think, Celeste. Think.

She turned toward the small terminal embedded in the cabin wall. It was still active, though barely—restricted access, minimal functions. Shaw had locked them out of major systems, but Celeste wasn't just any scientist. She knew her way around security loopholes.

She sat down in the chair, her fingers flying across the touch-screen. "Come on, V.E.G.A. Don't shut me out."

The AI did not respond. The ship had been eerily silent since the incident in the maintenance bay. Either V.E.G.A. had been manually shut down, or something had corrupted its programming. Neither option reassured her.

The screen flickered. A single access request popped up.

SECURITY OVERRIDE REQUESTED.

Celeste's stomach twisted. Someone was trying to get into the system. But who?

Before she could analyze it further, a soft tap sounded against the ventilation panel above her bed.

She froze.

Her eyes snapped to the grate, the dim light barely illuminating the slits in the metal. It was too dark to see anything beyond.

Another tap.

Slow. Measured.

Celeste's breath caught in her throat. She reached for the small emergency multitool strapped to her belt and flipped open the plasma cutter. Her heart pounded as she stepped forward.

Then—a whisper.

"Celeste."

Her blood ran cold.

That voice.

It wasn't Orion.

And it wasn't human.

The hairs on the back of her neck stood up. She swallowed hard, forcing herself to stay rational, to focus.

"Who's there?" she whispered, her voice barely audible.

Silence.

Then—a shadow shifted behind the vent.

Celeste lunged backward just as the metal grate ripped from the wall, torn away as if by an unseen force. The vent was empty, a yawning void of darkness.

But something had been there.

She stumbled back toward the terminal, her breath coming in rapid gasps. She needed to get out. Now.

The cabin door was locked. But the vents—

Celeste turned back to the opening.

She had two choices. Stay trapped and wait for whatever was stalking her, or crawl into the darkness and face it on her own terms.

She didn't have to think twice.

With a deep breath, she pulled herself up into the vent, the metal biting into her palms as she navigated the narrow passageway. The artificial hum of the ship pulsed around her, vibrating through the confined space.

Then, from somewhere deeper inside the vents, she heard it.

Breathing.

Not hers.

Slow. Deliberate.

Celeste gritted her teeth, pushing forward. The vent branched in several directions, but she knew the layout of the Stellar Dawn by heart. If she could just make it to Orion's cabin—

A metallic clatter echoed behind her.

Celeste's entire body went rigid.

It was following her.

She moved faster, ignoring the sting of her scraped palms. The vents twisted and turned, the air thick with the scent of scorched metal and something else—something faintly organic. The taste of copper coated the back of her throat.

Then, just ahead—a faint glow.

She reached the next vent opening and peered through the slits. Orion's cabin.

He was standing near the door, his arms braced against the wall, his expression locked in deep concentration. He was working on the security override, unaware of what was moving above him.

Celeste exhaled. "Orion," she whispered.

He tensed, then turned sharply, his gaze snapping toward the vent. The second he saw her, his entire body relaxed—but only slightly.

"Celeste?" His voice was low, urgent.

She reached for the panel and shoved it open. "We need to get out of here. Now."

Orion didn't hesitate. He caught her as she dropped down, his arms strong, steady. The moment their bodies met, a spark rippled through her, a visceral reminder of their earlier kiss.

But there was no time for that now.

"Something's in the vents," she panted, pulling away. "I don't know what it is, but it's not human."

Orion's jaw tightened. "I figured as much."

She frowned. "What do you mean?"

He gestured toward his terminal. "I got into the system before they locked me out. There's a restricted section in the security logs. Someone—one of the crew—has been erasing records, manipulating footage."

Celeste's stomach twisted. "Shaw."

Orion nodded. "Or someone working with him."

A metallic clang rang out from inside the vent behind them.

They both turned.

Something was moving inside. Fast.

"Run," Orion ordered.

They bolted.

Orion forced the cabin door open with a manual override, and they slipped into the corridor, moving swiftly through the dim emergency lighting.

The ship felt different now. The silence was heavier, the air charged, as if the station itself was holding its breath.

Celeste didn't know where they were going—only that they couldn't stop.

Orion grabbed her wrist, his grip firm, his pace relentless. "We need to get to the control deck. If we can access the mainframe, we can find out what the hell is happening before they stop us."

Celeste nodded, but her mind was still racing. If someone had been manipulating the records, then that meant—

A terrifying thought slammed into her.

"What if we're not the only ones being hunted?" she whispered.

Orion slowed, turning toward her. His gaze was sharp, calculating. "What are you saying?"

Celeste exhaled. "What if it's not just us? What if someone on this crew isn't just covering up the truth—what if they're working with whatever is on this ship?"

Orion's eyes darkened. "Then we're running out of time."

The corridor lights flickered violently.

Then, from the end of the hallway—

A silhouette.

Standing perfectly still.

Orion froze. His grip on Celeste tightened.

Then, in a slow, jerking motion, the figure stepped forward.

Celeste's breath hitched.

It was Rhys.

And he was smiling.

Eight

Love on the Run

R hys Calloway should not have been standing there.

Celeste's breath came fast and uneven as she locked eyes with the impossible figure at the end of the corridor. The man she had seen floating lifeless in the airlock, his face frozen in terror, was now standing perfectly still, his lips curled into a hollow, unnatural smile.

Orion's hand tightened around her wrist. He wasn't moving, but she could feel the tension radiating off him like a coiled wire, ready to snap.

"Stay behind me," he murmured.

Celeste barely heard him over the roar of blood in her ears. Every instinct screamed at her to run, but her body felt locked in place.

Then, Rhys moved.

Not walked—moved.

His body glitched, a stuttered, unnatural motion as if space itself had rewound him a fraction of a second before forcing him forward again.

Celeste inhaled sharply, stepping back without thinking. Orion's grip on her wrist broke, but he was already stepping in front of her, his other hand reaching for the knife at his belt.

The hallway was silent except for the distant hum of the Stellar Dawn's failing power systems. The lights flickered, casting Rhys's too-wide grin into sharp, unnatural relief.

Then he spoke.

"You're not supposed to be here."

His voice didn't match his lips. It came a fraction of a second too late, like a corrupted audio file trying to sync with a video.

Orion tensed. "Celeste, move. Now."

She forced her legs to obey, stepping back toward the nearest corridor junction. But the second she moved, Rhys moved too— his body snapping forward in an instant, as if he had teleported halfway down the hall.

Celeste gasped, heart pounding. "Orion—"

"Run," Orion commanded.

They bolted.

Celeste sprinted down the corridor, her boots slamming against the floor panels, her breath coming in sharp bursts. Orion was right beside her, matching her pace, his hand brushing against hers in fleeting, desperate touches as they ran.

Behind them, the sound of static filled the air—an electrical crackling, as if the ship itself were trying to process an error.

Celeste risked a glance over her shoulder.

Rhys was gone.

She sucked in a breath, her throat raw from fear. "Orion, where did he—"

"I don't know."

The hallway ahead curved sharply toward the emergency access bay, where they could reroute power to the bridge—if it wasn't locked down.

But just as they reached the junction, the ship shifted.

A pulse, like something alive, rippled through the walls. The lights flickered red, then white, then dimmed altogether.

Then, the doors in front of them slammed shut.

Orion cursed, skidding to a stop. He spun around, his knife still gripped in his hand. Celeste turned too, her chest rising and falling in quick, shallow breaths.

The hallway was empty.

But they weren't alone.

A whisper slithered through the darkness, curling against the edges of her consciousness like a half-formed thought.

"You should have stayed asleep."

Celeste swallowed hard, pressing a hand to her temple. The voice wasn't outside her head. It was inside it.

Orion grabbed her hand. "Look at me."

She did. His green eyes were sharp, steady. A lifeline in the chaos unraveling around them.

"Do not listen to it." His voice was low, but firm. "It's not real. Not yet."

Not yet.

The words sent another shudder through her.

A sharp bang echoed from the corridor behind them. The

emergency bulkheads had sealed off their escape routes, leaving them trapped in a narrow, dimly lit section of the ship.

Celeste clenched her jaw. "We need to override the lockdown."

Orion exhaled, nodding. "The access panel's three doors down. I'll—"

Then, suddenly—

A hand grabbed his ankle.

Celeste screamed as Orion was yanked off balance, his body slamming against the floor with a force that sent a tremor through the metal panels.

A shadow was crawling from beneath the grated floor.

Rhys.

Or what used to be Rhys.

His body twitched violently, his limbs contorting at unnatural angles as he pulled himself up, his hands too fast against the metal. His mouth opened—a hollow, soundless scream—his jaw distending too far.

Orion kicked hard, breaking the thing's grip. He rolled onto his back, knife flashing in his hand, and stabbed downward.

The blade sank into flesh, but Rhys didn't even react.

Celeste didn't think—she moved, grabbing Orion by the shoulders and yanking him backward.

"Get up!" she gasped.

Orion was already scrambling to his feet, but the moment they turned to run, the corridor itself shifted.

The walls… breathed.

The metal stretched outward, forming indentations—handprints, faces, twisting shapes pressing against the panels from the inside.

The ship was becoming something else.

Celeste's mind screamed against the impossibility of it, but her body kept moving. Orion's fingers curled around hers, pulling her along, anchoring her to something real.

The emergency access panel was just ahead.

Orion reached it first, slamming his hand against the manual override. The screen flashed red, resisting his command.

Celeste's heart pounded. No, no, no.

"It's locked out," Orion muttered.

She moved beside him, fingers flying over the keypad, forcing a secondary bypass. Her clearance wasn't enough to shut down the full lockdown, but if she could—

A loud wail erupted from behind them.

Celeste turned—

Rhys was on the ceiling.

His body hung suspended in zero gravity, his limbs splayed unnaturally, his head tilted at an impossible angle. His eyes locked onto hers.

Then, he dropped.

Orion reacted first, grabbing Celeste and shoving her out of the way just as Rhys crashed onto the floor where she had stood.

Celeste hit the wall hard, the impact knocking the air from her lungs. Orion twisted, his knife ready—

But Rhys wasn't moving anymore.

His body lay in the center of the corridor, still and lifeless, as if nothing had happened.

Celeste coughed, pushing herself upright. "What the hell is happening?"

Orion's jaw was clenched tight, his breath ragged. "It's not just the ship. It's us."

She stared at him. "What do you mean?"

He hesitated. Then—slowly—he reached up and pressed two fingers against the side of his head.

Celeste followed his lead.

And froze.

Beneath her fingertips, she could feel it.

A pulse.

Not her own.

Not Orion's.

Something inside her skull, beating in rhythm with the ship.

Orion's voice was barely a whisper.

"We're changing."

Nine

The Truth Among the Stars

Celeste Arden sat in the dim glow of the emergency lights, pressing trembling fingers against the side of her skull. The pulse beneath her skin was faint, but unmistakable—a rhythm that didn't belong to her.

Not her heartbeat. Not Orion's.

Something else.

Her breath came in short, uneven bursts. Across from her, Orion sat with his back against the wall, his head tilted slightly, his own fingers still resting against his temple. His green eyes, sharp even in the low light, flickered with something dark. Something he wasn't saying.

She swallowed hard. "Tell me I'm imagining this."

He didn't answer right away.

That was enough of an answer.

Celeste exhaled sharply, dropping her hand. The air in the corridor was heavy, thick with an invisible weight, pressing down on them like an unseen force. The faint, metallic tang of blood still clung to her tongue, but whether it was from Rhys, the ship, or something else entirely, she didn't know.

Orion finally spoke, his voice low. Controlled.

"It started before today."

Celeste's pulse spiked. "What do you mean?"

He hesitated, running a hand through his dark hair. "Ever since we got close to V-616C, something's been… off. At first, I thought it was just the ship. Minor malfunctions, weird glitches in the logs. Then I started noticing time skips. Gaps in my memory. Minutes—sometimes whole hours—where I'd find myself standing somewhere with no idea how I got there."

Celeste's breath hitched. "That's impossible."

Orion's gaze locked onto hers. "Then explain why you've been doing the same thing."

A sharp chill ran down her spine. "That's not—"

But even as she said it, she knew he was right.

She thought back to the past few days. The restless nights. The sense of waking up but not remembering falling asleep. The hours spent in the research bay where she'd stare at her logs, feeling like she had missed something crucial but couldn't place what.

Had she lost time? Had she changed without even realizing it?

She forced herself to meet Orion's gaze. "Why didn't you tell me sooner?"

A muscle in his jaw tensed. "Because I didn't want to believe it. And because—" His voice lowered slightly. "You're the only person on this ship I trust."

The words hit her like an electric shock.

Orion Vale was a man of secrets. Of closed doors and calculated words. But right now, there was nothing guarded in his expression. Just something raw.

Something terrifying.

Celeste's chest tightened. "Then we need to figure out what's happening. Before—" She hesitated. "Before we become whatever Rhys was."

Orion nodded, pushing off the wall and rising to his feet. He reached down, offering her his hand. Without hesitation, she took it. His fingers curled around hers, solid and real, and for a brief second, she let herself hold onto that.

Then the hallway lights flickered violently.

A loud crack rang through the ship—metal groaning, as if the Stellar Dawn itself was resisting something unseen.

Celeste whipped around, her heart hammering. "What was that?"

Orion didn't answer. He was already moving, pulling her with him. "Come on."

They sprinted down the corridor, their footfalls barely registering beneath the rising hum of the ship. Every flickering light, every glitching panel, every warped shadow felt like it was watching them.

Then—a voice crackled through the comms.

"Approaching Phase Three."

Celeste skidded to a stop, her stomach dropping. The voice was calm. Methodical.

She turned to Orion. "Phase Three?"

His expression darkened. "I've never heard that before."

A sinking feeling took root in Celeste's chest. If Phase Three was something built into the ship's systems, that meant someone had planned this.

Someone knew this would happen.

And someone was watching it unfold.

They reached the control deck doors, but as Orion went to punch in the override, the screen flashed red.

ACCESS DENIED.

Orion cursed. "They locked us out."

Celeste's mind raced. "Not entirely." She dropped to her knees, prying open the emergency panel beneath the main console. Inside was a secondary access core—a manual bypass for system failures. She yanked out the exposed wires, her fingers moving fast.

"Can you hack it?" Orion asked, crouching beside her.

"I can force a temporary override, but it won't last long."

Orion pulled a knife from his belt, flipping it in his fingers before jamming the tip into the base of the access panel. Sparks flew, and the screen flickered.

MANUAL OVERRIDE INITIATED.

Celeste exhaled. "We're in."

The doors hissed open.

They slipped inside, the control deck bathed in red warning lights. The large front windows looked out over the dark expanse of space, V-616C looming below, its swirling storms violent and mesmerizing.

Orion immediately moved to the central console, scanning through system logs. Celeste turned to another monitor, pulling up restricted transmissions.

Then, she found it.

A video feed.

She pressed play.

A recording flickered to life on the screen.

At first, it was static. Then, an image emerged.

Celeste felt her stomach drop.

The screen showed a previous crew aboard the Stellar Dawn.

Their uniforms were different—older. But their faces were filled with the same fear Celeste felt now.

Then the camera glitched—and Celeste recognized someone.

Orion.

Orion Vale.

Her breath caught. "Orion—"

He turned sharply, his eyes narrowing at the screen.

It was him. Standing alongside a crew she had never seen before. His expression was grim, his stance rigid. The timestamp in the corner showed a date far older than it should have been.

"Orion," she whispered. "How is this possible?"

His face was unreadable.

Then, in the recording, another figure appeared behind him.

Celeste's blood turned to ice.

The figure was her.

The screen flickered violently, the image breaking apart.

Then—one final message appeared.

THIS HAS HAPPENED BEFORE.

The control deck shook violently, the lights flaring blinding white. Celeste stumbled into Orion, her pulse skyrocketing.

The ship was reacting.

As if it knew they had found the truth.

Orion caught her, his arms wrapping around her to steady her. His breath was hot against her ear. "We're running out of time."

Celeste looked up at him, her heart pounding. Nothing made sense anymore.

Except one thing.

The way he held onto her like he'd done it a thousand times before.

Like he knew her.

Like he had always known her.

The ship lurched, alarms blaring.

And Celeste realized—

They were never meant to leave this place alive.

Ten

Between Love and Survival

The Stellar Dawn lurched violently, throwing Celeste off balance. She slammed into the console, barely managing to brace herself against the cold metal as alarms blared overhead. The control deck lights flashed between red and white, the ship's systems in chaos.

Orion caught her before she could fall, his arms wrapping around her waist, his grip tight. His breath was warm against her temple, but his voice was sharp.

"We need to move. Now."

Celeste's mind was still reeling. The recording—that impossible recording—was burned into her brain. A past crew. A past them.

"This has happened before."

The words echoed in her skull, a cruel whisper curling around her thoughts.

She looked up at Orion, her pulse roaring in her ears. "Tell me you remember something. Anything."

Orion's jaw clenched, his expression a mixture of urgency and something deeper—something haunted. "Not completely. Just… flashes." His fingers curled against her waist, grounding himself. "I don't know how, but we've been here before, Celeste."

Celeste's throat tightened.

The moment stretched between them, heavy, unspoken things hanging in the air like static charge before a storm.

Then—

The ship shifted again.

The deck pitched sideways, metal groaning under stress. The gravitational stabilizers flickered, sending a sudden weightlessness through the air. Celeste gasped as she was pulled upward, her body floating before Orion caught her again, anchoring her.

He pulled her close, their bodies colliding as they tumbled, gravity failing them both.

His voice was tight against her ear. "Hold onto me."

Celeste did.

Then, the lights went out.

Total darkness swallowed them.

For a long, terrifying moment, there was only the distant sound of their breathing, the faint crackling of the failing ship's systems. The vast, suffocating silence of space pressed in around them.

Celeste's fingers dug into Orion's flight suit, her breath shallow.

Then—

A voice.

"You should have left it alone."

Celeste froze.

The voice didn't come from the comms.

It came from inside the room.

Orion twisted, pulling a small tactical light from his belt and flashing it toward the entrance.

The beam landed on something standing just inside the doorway.

Celeste sucked in a breath.

It was Captain Shaw.

But—not.

His body was wrong, his arms slightly too long, his head tilted at a sickening angle. His uniform was tattered, darkened with what looked like blood. His eyes—

Celeste's stomach lurched.

His eyes were completely black.

No irises. No whites. Just an abyss staring back at her.

Orion tensed beside her. "Shaw—?"

Shaw's lips twitched into a too-wide grin.

Then he moved.

Celeste barely had time to react before he lunged, inhumanly fast, crossing the space in a heartbeat.

Orion shoved Celeste out of the way just as Shaw's arm swung toward him. The impact sent Orion crashing into the console, his knife skidding across the floor.

Celeste's breath caught in her throat.

Shaw turned to her.

His mouth opened, but the sound that came out wasn't human—it was a garbled, static-laced distortion, as if a radio signal had fused with something organic.

Celeste moved on instinct.

She grabbed the nearest metal panel and swung hard. The impact landed against Shaw's shoulder, but he barely flinched.

His head snapped toward her—jerky, unnatural movements—before he grabbed her wrist with an iron grip.

Pain shot up her arm.

Orion was already moving, back on his feet. He lunged, grabbing Shaw by the collar and yanking him backward, his strength fueled by something deeper than adrenaline.

Shaw hissed—a broken, static sound—as Orion threw him to the floor.

"Celeste—go!"

Celeste didn't hesitate. She grabbed Orion's hand, pulling him toward the emergency hatch leading to the bridge's secondary control room.

Behind them, Shaw's body twitched violently, his limbs spasming.

Then—he started laughing.

The sound was wrong. A distorted echo of something human, but twisted into something else.

Celeste's breath shook, but she kept running.

They stumbled into the secondary control room, Orion slamming the hatch shut behind them.

Celeste collapsed against the wall, her chest rising and falling rapidly.

Orion braced against the console, his knuckles white as he gripped the edge. He turned to her, his eyes dark, searching.

"You okay?"

Celeste let out a shaky breath. "No."

A beat of silence. Then, despite everything, Orion let out a breathless, almost humorless chuckle.

Celeste narrowed her eyes. "Did you just—laugh?"

Orion exhaled, dragging a hand down his face. "I think I'm losing my mind."

Celeste stared at him for a second. Then—she did something completely irrational.

She reached for his hand, lacing her fingers through his.

Orion stilled.

His pulse pounded beneath her touch.

He looked down at their joined hands, then back at her. For a long, unspoken second, it was just them.

No ship. No voices. No monsters.

Just this moment.

Celeste's voice was quiet. Fragile. "I don't know what's happening to us."

Orion's grip on her tightened. "We'll figure it out."

His voice was steady. But there was something else in it now.

A promise.

Celeste swallowed hard, something aching in her chest. She had never let herself be vulnerable, had never let herself need anyone.

But right now—

Right now, she needed him.

And she had a feeling she always had.

A low hum vibrated through the ship.

Orion pulled her closer. "We need to move."

Celeste nodded. "Then let's end this."

She didn't know where this road would lead. Didn't know if they'd survive.

But if she was going to face the unknown, if she was going to fight against whatever force was rewriting their existence—

She wasn't doing it alone.

Eleven

The Ultimate Sacrifice

The Stellar Dawn trembled beneath their feet as Celeste and Orion made their way through the dimly lit corridors, their every step echoing in the silence that had swallowed the ship. The warning alarms had died down, but the stillness had only deepened, thickened the air, leaving an unnatural heaviness in its wake. Each corner they turned seemed to close in on them, the ship itself twisting and stretching like something alive, something that wanted to keep them trapped inside its hull forever.

Orion's hand was warm in hers, but even that comfort felt fragile, like it might disappear at any moment. The pull between them, the charge in the air, was undeniable, but it was buried beneath the suffocating dread of what was happening around them.

They reached the end of the hall where a darkened bulkhead waited, locked tight. The last access point before they could reach the main bridge, the heart of the ship's operations. But the security panel beside the door flickered erratically, the red light blinking like a pulse—too erratic to be natural.

Orion's fingers brushed against the panel, the quiet hiss of the override system reverberating around them. "It's locked down tight," he muttered, his voice low but intense. "We need to find another way in."

Celeste barely heard him. The pulse at the back of her mind—the same pulse that had plagued her since the moment they found themselves at the heart of this nightmare—was growing louder. She pressed her palm against her temple, feeling the rhythm that wasn't her own, that wasn't Orion's. Something deeper. Something familiar.

"What if we can't get through?" she asked, her voice thick with the weight of the question. It wasn't just a technical issue anymore. It was a matter of survival.

Orion stopped and turned to face her, his expression unreadable, but his eyes—they were full of knowing. "Then we find another way."

His hand reached for her wrist, the warmth of his fingers grounding her in the moment. The intensity in his gaze was unmistakable. There was something deep inside of him—something she could no longer ignore.

The air between them seemed to crackle, the tension too thick to cut. Celeste had been fighting it, fighting the pull between them, for days now. But in this moment, with the ship falling apart around them, with death itself lurking just beyond their reach, she couldn't deny it any longer.

She needed him.

She needed him in a way that terrified her.

Orion stepped closer, his breath warm against her ear. "Celeste," he murmured, his voice a soft growl in the silence.

Her pulse quickened. She swallowed hard, trying to steady herself, but the closeness, the weight of their shared understanding, was overwhelming. "What if we can't make it out?" she whispered. "What if…" Her throat tightened. She couldn't say the words. Couldn't give life to the fear that had been creeping into her chest ever since they first encountered the presence inside the ship.

Orion cupped her face gently, his thumb brushing across her cheek. "We'll make it out. Together."

His words were an anchor in the storm that had become their lives. She searched his eyes, seeking the truth in them, needing to believe him.

And then, without thinking, without hesitation, she kissed him.

The moment their lips met, the world seemed to disappear.

The tension, the fear, the unknowns—they melted away. It was just the two of them, their bodies pressed together, their hearts beating in sync, their breaths mingling in the stillness.

Orion's arms wrapped around her waist, pulling her closer, deepening the kiss. She could feel the heat in his touch, the strength in his body, and for the first time in what felt like forever, she allowed herself to feel. To need.

It was raw, and it was everything they had been denying. In that kiss, there were no walls, no secrets, no space between them. Just two people clinging to what they had left.

Then—

The ship shuddered beneath their feet, the low groan of the hull filling the silence between them.

The kiss broke, both of them pulling away, breathing heavily.

"We need to move," Orion said, his voice hoarse. His hands were still gripping her, as if he couldn't quite let go. But his eyes—his eyes were filled with something darker now. Something that Celeste couldn't fully decipher.

She nodded, forcing her thoughts back into focus. There was no time for weakness, no time for hesitation. They were running out of time.

But as they turned to the locked bulkhead, the door shuddered again, the lights above flickering as if the ship itself was warning them.

And then—a sound.

A voice.

Celeste froze.

"Orion."

His name was a whisper, but it felt as though it was spoken directly into her mind.

Orion's hand tightened around hers, his body going still beside her. "Did you hear that?" he asked, his voice barely above a whisper.

Celeste's heart skipped a beat. "It's not just us."

She turned, her eyes scanning the dim corridor behind them. The air felt wrong—too still, too heavy. And then she saw it.

A figure.

Shadows.

The outline of a person—tall, dressed in the same tattered uniform as the crew, their face obscured by the blackened haze of the flickering lights.

And then, the voice again.

"Come closer."

The words felt like a command, pulling at something deep inside Celeste, urging her forward. But she resisted, her pulse thundering in her ears.

"No," she said firmly, her voice shaking but defiant.

Orion's grip tightened on her wrist, pulling her back. "It's not real," he whispered urgently. "It can't be."

But Celeste knew. This wasn't a hallucination. The presence was real. It had been inside the ship since they first stepped foot aboard. Watching. Waiting.

The figure stepped forward, its face still obscured. But as it moved into the light, the familiar eyes came into view.

Shaw.

His body was bent unnaturally, his arms stretching too far, his face twisted into something inhuman.

"Come closer," Shaw repeated, his voice not his own. It was the same distorted static, a crackling that broke and reformed with each word.

Orion pulled Celeste close, pushing her behind him. "Stay back," he warned.

But Shaw didn't listen. His body jerked forward, his arms

outstretched, as if the very ship itself was pushing him toward them.

The walls seemed to pulse, the floor shifting beneath them as if the Stellar Dawn was coming alive in a way neither of them could understand.

Orion stepped forward, his hand still firmly gripping Celeste's, his voice low but resolute. "Stay here."

Celeste opened her mouth to protest, but the ship's hum increased in volume, drowning out her words. Orion's eyes flashed with something dark and desperate. "We don't have a choice."

He pushed her toward the bulkhead, toward the final barrier between them and the truth.

Celeste stumbled, her heart racing. She didn't want to lose him. She didn't want to lose them.

Orion looked back, his eyes filled with an emotion she couldn't place. And then, just as Shaw's outstretched hands reached for them—

The airlock doors slammed shut.

They were sealed inside.

The final choice had been made.

Twelve

The Final Confrontation

The Stellar Dawn shuddered again, a violent tremor that rattled through the ship's skeletal frame. The emergency lights, flickering erratically, painted the corridors with sickly flashes of red and white, casting long, grotesque shadows against the walls. The air was thick—heavy with the smell of ozone, oil, and something unnervingly organic. It pressed in on Celeste Arden from all sides, suffocating her, as if the ship itself were alive, closing in on them.

She could feel it now—the pulse, that low, insistent thrum beneath her skin, like a heartbeat not her own. It had been there, ever since they first boarded, growing louder with every passing moment, becoming more difficult to ignore. Whatever this was, whatever had brought them to the edge of destruction, it wasn't just the ship. It was in them.

Orion's grip on her hand was firm, his fingers tightening around hers as he led her through the maze of twisting corridors, the steady hum of machinery and distorted voices echoing around them. His breath was ragged, his body tense, as if he were bracing for an impact they both knew was inevitable.

"We need to stop it, Celeste," he said, his voice barely more than a whisper, but the urgency in it sent a shiver through her. He stopped in front of the door to the main control room, his eyes fixed on the hatch. She could see the unspoken pain in his gaze. The ship wasn't just something to escape—it was something they had been drawn into. "We can't let it take us. We have to finish this."

Celeste swallowed the lump in her throat. She could feel it too. The pull, the pull of something so much larger than them. Something predetermined. The truth they had uncovered was more horrifying than either of them could have imagined. They were part of it, part of the cycle that had already been written. But somehow, they had to break it.

With a sharp exhale, she nodded. "We don't have a choice."

Orion pressed the manual override, but the door didn't budge. The ship's defenses were tightened, a final, desperate attempt to keep them out. The walls seemed to breathe, warping and shifting under some foreign pressure.

"We have to make a choice," he said, his voice harsh with emotion.

Her gaze locked with his. The connection between them was undeniable now. It wasn't just the shared terror that bound them. It wasn't just the physical attraction, the impossible chemistry between them. It was something deeper. Something that couldn't be ignored any longer.

The moments that had felt like a dream, when she had questioned everything about herself and her past—all of it was leading to this. The pulse inside her wasn't just an external force—it was part of her. It had always been part of her.

Orion's grip on her hand tightened. His eyes searched hers, his face set with determination. "If we don't stop it now, there won't be anyone left. The ship—it's alive, Celeste. We have to sever the connection before it uses us."

It was all too much. The pressure. The terror. The uncertainty. But even so, she stepped closer to him, her voice shaking only slightly. "What happens if we can't stop it?"

"We die," he answered, but there was no fear in his tone. Only resolve. His lips brushed the top of her head in a gentle, fleeting kiss, a soft promise in the midst of the madness. "But not without a fight."

Her heart twisted. She nodded, determined to follow him. They were in this together now, for better or worse.

Orion reached for the override once again. His fingers hovered over the controls. A deep hum surged through the ship, reverberating through the walls as if something was responding to their actions.

There was a sudden, sharp crack—the door's seal gave way with a groaning protest, sliding open into the unknown. The air that rushed in felt wrong—thick with static and a bitter scent she couldn't identify. The main control room lay beyond, bathed in the same sickly red light that had been haunting them for days.

Inside, the center of the ship was laid bare. The heart of the Stellar Dawn.

The room stretched out in a way that seemed impossible, as if the walls themselves were not just physical boundaries but were distorting the very fabric of space. The control panels were flickering, lines of code flashing too quickly to follow. At the center of it all stood a figure—a shadow, tall and dark, a silhouette that seemed to move in and out of focus.

A whisper slid through the air, coming from nowhere and everywhere at once. "You shouldn't have come."

It wasn't a voice anymore. It was a presence, something so deeply embedded in the ship that it was no longer human. Celeste's skin crawled, and she pulled away from Orion instinctively, as if the voice was touching her from the inside out.

The figure stepped forward. Shaw.

But this time, he wasn't just a man. He was something else, something other. The shadows clung to him, warping his form, twisting his features into something unrecognizable, something inhuman.

Celeste's breath caught in her throat. "Shaw?" Her voice was small, but the echo of it seemed to reverberate across the entire room, bouncing off the walls, lost in the twisting air.

The figure smiled—that same too-wide smile—but his eyes, black as the void, focused on them with terrifying clarity. "You're too late. It's already begun."

Orion stepped in front of her, his body blocking her from the figure's gaze. His voice was low, commanding. "No. We'll end it here."

The shadow flickered. The air in the room grew dense with an almost palpable force, like a living thing pressing against their skin. Shaw's voice came again, but it was distorted, like a radio signal turning in and out of focus. "You think you can stop it? You can't. The Stellar Dawn is already a part of you. The cycle cannot be broken."

Celeste's heart hammered in her chest. The walls seemed to close in, warping and twisting as the air thickened, like the ship itself was trying to swallow them whole. "We'll see about that." Her voice was a quiet defiance, but it was enough. Enough to push forward.

Orion moved beside her, and without another word, he lunged at the central console. The ship shuddered again, the entire structure groaning under the pressure. The shadows around

Shaw seemed to distort, elongating as though trying to reach out, to drag them back into the dark.

Celeste reached for the manual override. She could feel it now—the pulse that was inside her, thrumming beneath her ribs, in perfect rhythm with the ship. It was as though she was connected to it, as though the Stellar Dawn's heartbeat was hers.

The screens in front of them flared to life as the system code began to decode itself, lines of data flashing, revealing the true core of the ship's design—its purpose.

Orion's voice cut through the chaos. "We can do this, Celeste. We can stop it." His hand found hers, his fingers locking around hers, as if to pull her into the present, to anchor her to something real.

Shaw's form flickered again, his laughter echoing through the room, raw and ragged. "You're fools. The ship is more than just a vessel. It is a legacy. A prison. And now—" His voice dropped to a cold, final whisper. "It will have you both."

Celeste felt it—the pulse—surging. It was inside her and the ship. She understood now. They had always been part of the cycle, from the very beginning. The ship was not a machine. It was alive. It had chosen them.

And now, they had to choose. They had to stop it. Or let it consume them.

Orion squeezed her hand tighter. "Celeste… we end this."

And in that moment, they made their choice. Together.

The pulse between them surged, reaching out into the heart of the ship, overwhelming the controls, breaking the cycle. The shadows around Shaw screamed in agony, as the connection was severed.

And as the Stellar Dawn screamed in protest, they knew: the battle was far from over. But at least—for now—they had each other.

9 784569 529370